Nelson English

Developing Non-fiction Skills

BOOK TWO 2

John Jackman   Wendy Wren

Nelson

Contents

Unit	DEVELOPMENT — Text	SKILLS — Word	
1 Vikings	Invasion!	Suffixes	Homophones
2 China	The Great Wall of China	Using a dictionary	Verbs – adding 'ing' and 'ed'
3 Flood	Disaster	Synonyms	Changing verb tenses
4 Fireworks	Bonfire Night	Using nouns as verbs and verbs as nouns	Homophones
5 Castles	What is a Siege?	Old and new words	Syllables
6 Rubbish	Recycling	Over-used words – 'nice'	'le', 'al' and 'el' word endings
7 Bridges	Books about Bridges	Definitions	Using a dictionary
8 Snow Stories	Footprints	Making adjectives	'dge' letter pattern
9 Roald Dahl	A Famous Author	Using a thesaurus	Root words
10 Fire	Fire Beneath our Feet	Synonyms	It's or its?
11 India	Holidays in India	Similes	Suffix 'ion'
12 Country Pursuits	Fishing	Homonyms	Root words, prefixes and suffixes
Check-up			

SKILLS		DEVELOPMENT	Pages
Sentence		Text	
Choosing verbs	Capital letters	Newspaper reports	4
Verb tenses	Ending sentences	Factual writing	10
Adverbs	Speech marks	Fact and opinion	16
Verb tenses	Special uses of capital letters	Instructions	22
Pairs of adjectives	Apostrophes for possession	Explanations	28
Adjective phrases	Apostrophes for possession	Information text	34
Adjectives	Word order	Collecting information	40
Adverbs	Clauses and phrases	Fact and opinion	46
Adjectives and adverbs	Setting out a letter	Writing to persuade	52
Nouns and verbs	Punctuating sentences	Summaries	58
Future-tense verbs	Positive and negative sentences	Advertisements	64
Word classes	Using 'who' and 'which'	Points of view	70
			76

Unit 1 Vikings — Invasion!

Viking Invasion!

by Thomas Scribe

Last night, villagers around the mouth of the River Thames witnessed a frightening spectacle. After a brief period of peace, trouble looked about to flare up again. Just as the sun was setting, a fleet of over 100 Viking longboats appeared over the horizon, rowing at full speed towards London.

As I watched, there were farmers running home, driving their cattle, hoping not to be the next victims of these fierce warriors. Women were crying and hurrying their children to safety.

One man who was willing to stop and speak to me was obviously distraught. "Not again!" he said. "How many times are our villages going to be burnt? How many times must we run in fear of our lives before somebody will do something?"

This sighting of Viking ships, however, should not have been a total surprise. Speaking in London last month, King Alfred warned of a likely invasion by the Vikings. He made it clear that people should prepare themselves for Viking attacks this spring. His spies have heard that some Vikings, led by Guthrun, intend to land here and build forts, but the King has promised they won't have any of our land. He said we must arm ourselves and drive them away. We have a brave and bold leader in King Alfred, but these Vikings look a tough bunch.

On this occasion, the villagers in this area had a lucky escape. The Viking ships sailed on up the River Thames, heading straight for London. Once the ships had passed and the panic had died down, I was able to speak to the village chief about their lucky escape. "I don't think we've seen the last of those Vikings," he said. "They may have passed by this time, but if London cannot stand against them, we are doomed. If King Alfred and his army are defeated, how long do you think it will be before more Vikings come sailing over the horizon?" How long indeed? We can only watch and wait.

Comprehension

A Write a sentence to answer each question.
1. What happened 'just as the sun was setting'?
2. What did the farmers do?
3. How did King Alfred know what the Vikings were planning?
4. How does the writer describe King Alfred?

B Write down what each of the following phrases means. Use a dictionary or a thesaurus to help you.
1. a frightening spectacle
2. a brief period of peace
3. obviously distraught
4. on this occasion
5. we are doomed

C
1. Do you think the newspaper article has an eye-catching headline? Explain your reasons.
2. Why do you think the reporter wanted to speak to one of the villagers?
3. Why do you think the reporter has included an illustration?
4. Make a list of the facts in the newspaper report.
5. Write down an example of an opinion in the newspaper report.

flee in terror as the longboats come into view.

Vocabulary
Suffixes

The words in the following pairs are similar because they are from the same word family, but they have different **suffixes**.

inva<u>sion</u>	inv<u>ade</u>
terri<u>ble</u>	ter<u>rify</u>
crea<u>tion</u>	cre<u>ate</u>

Remember, a **suffix** is a word ending.

A 1 Add the suffix 'ify' or 'ate' to each group of letters to make a word.

a horr____ b educ____ c oper____

d ident____ e irrit____ f simpl____

2 For each word below, make a new word that ends with 'ate' and is from the same word family. The first one has been done to help you.

a navigation   *navigate*
b cultivation   c calculation   d acceleration
e situation   f evaporation   g congratulation
h agitation   i anticipation j regulation

B 1 Invent a spelling rule about how you changed the words in question 2 of part A.

2 Choose three of the 'ate' words that you made in part A and use each one in a sentence of your own.

Spelling
Homophones

Remember, **homophones** are words that sound the same but are spelt differently and have different meanings. For example:
<u>There</u> were farmers driving <u>their</u> cattle home.

One word has two homophones!

A Copy each word below and write a homophone next to it. The first one has been done to help you.

1 beech   *beach*

2 flour   3 hare   4 hear   5 know

6 too   7 peace 8 sight 9 weight

B Use each pair of homophones in a sentence of your own.

1 blue   blew   2 threw   through

3 see   sea   4 heard   herd

Grammar

Choosing verbs

Choosing the best verb makes a sentence more interesting.

You need to think carefully about the best **verb** to use in a sentence. For example:

   Women were <u>hurrying</u> their children to safety.

Other verbs, like 'rushing', 'gathering', 'guiding' or 'urging' could have been used instead of 'hurrying'.

A Write three other verbs that have a similar meaning to each verb below.

1 speak   2 walk   3 shout   4 throw

B Write two other verbs that could have been used in place of the underlined word in each sentence.

1 Last night, villagers <u>witnessed</u> a frightening spectacle.
2 There were farmers <u>running</u> home.
3 Women were <u>crying</u>.
4 They will <u>build</u> forts.

Punctuation

Capital letters

A **proper noun** is a special naming word.

Remember, we use a **capital letter**:
- to begin a sentence
- as the first letter of a proper noun
- as the first letter of important words in book, film or play titles
- for the word 'I'.

For example:
   <u>F</u>or homework, <u>E</u>mma and <u>I</u> read '<u>T</u>he <u>S</u>tory of the <u>V</u>ikings'.

A Write these sentences correctly, putting in the capital letters.

1 the vikings sailed up the river thames to london.
2 the vikings came from denmark, norway and sweden.
3 the reporter from the saxon daily news saw the viking longboat.
4 the viking attacks made king alfred angry.

 Remember, to use capital letters for all the proper nouns.

B Write a fact sheet like this:

Date of attack: _____
Name of invaders: _____
Name of river where longboat was seen: _____
Name of town attackers were heading for: _____
Name of leader of attackers: _____
Name of King of England: _____

 Writing

Newspaper reports

When you write a **newspaper report**, you should include:
- the facts – what actually happened
- eye-witness accounts – you can interview some of the people who saw or were part of the incident you are reporting
- background information – you may want to tell your readers about events that led up to what you are reporting.

Imagine you are a reporter, living at the time of a famous historical event. Choose an event you have learned about in your topic work, or one of these:
- the start of the Great Fire of London
- the day on which an Egyptian pyramid was completed
- the evacuation from London of a group of children during the Second World War.

Write a newspaper report about your chosen event. The diagram and notes opposite will help you plan your work.

Vikings unit 1

unit 1 Vikings

Name of your newspaper
You can use the name of a real newspaper or you can make one up.

Headline
This is very important. If people find the headline interesting or amusing they will want to read the report. If the reporter had just written 'Boat Seen' it would not have 'grabbed' the readers' attention.
For your headline you could use **alliteration** – having two or more words that start with the same sound, for example: 'Villagers View Vikings'.

Saxon Daily News
3rd March 871

Viking Invasion!

by Thomas Scribe

Last night, villagers around the mouth of the River Thames witnessed a frightening spectacle. After a brief period of peace, trouble looked about to flare up again. Just as the sun was setting, a fleet of over 100 Viking longboats appeared over the horizon, rowing at full speed towards London.

[...] running [...] to be the [...]. Women [...] children [...] stop and [...] ght. Not [...] es are our [...] many times [...] ves before [...], however, should not have been a total surprise. Speaking in London last month, King Alfred warned of a likely invasion by the Vikings. He made it clear that people should prepare themselves for Viking attacks this spring. His spies have heard that some Vikings, led by Guthrun, intend to land here and build forts, but the King has promised they won't have any of our land. He said we must arm ourselves and drive them away. We have a brave and bold leader in King Alfred, but these Vikings look a tough bunch.

On this occasion, the villagers in this area had a lucky escape. The Viking ships sailed on up the River Thames, heading straight for London. Once the ships had passed and the panic had died down, I was able to speak to the village chief about their lucky escape. "I don't think we've seen the last of those Vikings," he said. "They may have passed by this time, but if London cannot stand against them, we are doomed. If King Alfred and his army are defeated, how long do you think it will be before more Vikings come sailing over the horizon?" How long indeed? We can only watch and wait.

Reporter's name
The name of the reporter usually appears at the beginning of the story. This is called a **byline**. Use your own name or make one up.

Villagers flee in terror as the longboats come into view.

Illustration
A newspaper report is more interesting if there is a drawing or photograph to go with it. An illustration might show one of the main people mentioned in the report, the place where the event occurred or the event actually happening. Remember that your illustration should help the reader to understand the report.

Caption
A **caption** tells the reader what the illustration shows.

The Great Wall of China

Unforgettable China

If you are lucky enough to visit China then the Great Wall of China is not to be missed. Stretching nearly 6,000 km, the wall forms a barrier from the town of Gansu in the west to the Yellow Sea in the east. It continues to draw thousands of visitors every day, nearly 2,400 years after it was built.

Described as one of the Seven Wonders of the World, it is said to be the only human construction that is visible from the Moon! Visitors stand and stare in amazement, finding it hard to believe that such a structure could have been created in the third century BC. Emperor Qin Shihuangdi ordered the wall to be built to prevent invasions from the north. Such a wall needed gates for people and goods to pass through, and these gates became centres where towns grew up. In the end, it was one of these gates, opened by a traitor, that allowed the Manchu to invade, but not until over 1,000 years after the wall had been built!

If you ever have the opportunity to visit the Great Wall, it will be a truly unforgettable experience.

Comprehension

A Write a sentence to answer each question.

1. Where does the wall start in the west?
2. Where does it finish in the east?
3. Who ordered the wall to be built?
4. Why was the wall built?
5. How did the Manchu manage to invade China?

Fact File
The Great Wall of China

Location:
North-eastern China, along the Mongolian Plateau

When built:
220–210 BC

Time taken to build it:
10 years

Length:
approximately 5,500 km

Height:
6–15 m

Width:
4–12 m

China

Lookout tower

Ramparts

Comprehension

B Write a sentence to answer each question.

1. How long did the Great Wall of China take to build?
2. How high is it?
3. How long is it?
4. How wide is it?
5. When was it built?
6. Why do you think the height and width of the wall vary in places?

C Both these pieces of writing about the Great Wall of China are non-fiction. They both give the reader facts, but they are very different.

1. Which would you read if you wanted to know some basic facts about the Great Wall of China?
2. Which would you read if you were thinking of going on a holiday to China?
3. Do you think the pictures are useful? Explain your reasons.

Vocabulary

Using a dictionary

The words in a dictionary are in alphabetical order.

Remember, if you are sorting words into alphabetical order, and they begin with the same letter, you need to look at the second letter of each word. For example:

baboon   bear   birds   boar   buffalo
a b c d e f g h i j k l m n o p q r s t u v w x y z

If the second letters are the same, you need to look at the third letters. For example:

chair   chess   China   choir   chutney
a b c d e f g h i j k l m n o p q r s t u v w x y z

A Sort these words into alphabetical order.

1. chestnut   charcoal   churn   chicks
2. herd   heap   hexagon   help
3. month   moth   moss   mole
4. wall   warfare   wafer   wake

B 1 Write your own short definition of each of these words.

   a create   b awe   c traitor
   d visible   e invade   f location

2 Use a dictionary to find the correct definition of each word from question 1. Copy the definitions.

Spelling

Verbs – adding 'ing' and 'ed'

Remember, the **vowels** are: a, e, i, o and u. All other letters are **consonants**.

Remember, to add 'ing' to a short word, look at the letter before the last letter. If it is a consonant, just add 'ing'. If it is a single vowel, double the last letter and add 'ing'. But, if the letter before is a vowel too, just add 'ing'. For example:

sing   singing   hop   hopping   read   reading

| consonant | single vowel | double vowel letters |

For words ending in 'w', 'x' or 'y', **don't** double the last letter. For example:

draw   drawing   play   played

This rule also applies to adding 'ed'.

A Add 'ing' and then 'ed' to each of these verbs.

1 bat	2 pin	3 land	4 shout
5 tap	6 slip	7 flow	8 mend
9 rock	10 plug	11 drill	12 box

To add 'ing' or 'ed' to words that end with 'e', we usually remove the 'e' first. For example:

come   coming   live   lived

B Add 'ing' and then 'ed' to each of these verbs.

1 smile	2 rake	3 mime	4 skate
5 choke	6 wave	7 hope	8 dive
9 stroke	10 prune	11 live	12 share

 Grammar

Verb tenses

Remember, when we write about what is happening now, we use verbs in the **present tense**. For example:

The visitor <u>walks</u> along the wall.

or

The visitor <u>is</u> <u>walking</u> along the wall.

　　　　　　helper verb　　verb

When we write about something that has happened in the past, we use verbs in the **past tense**. For example:

The visitor <u>walked</u> along the wall.

or

The visitor <u>was</u> <u>walking</u> along the wall.

　　　　　　helper verb　　verb

Notice how both the present and the past tense can be written with 'helper' verbs.

A Copy and complete this table.

Verb family name	Present tense	Past tense
1 to walk	he walks	she walked
	they are walking	we were walking
2 to watch	I _____	we _____
	she _____ _____	they _____ _____
3 to visit	you _____	I _____
	he _____ _____	I _____ _____
4 to climb	we _____	he _____
	she _____ _____	they _____ _____
5 to stare	they _____	he _____
	I _____ _____	you _____ _____

B Copy the sentences below. Change the verbs from the present tense to the past tense.

1. The guide explains the history of the Great Wall.
2. She tells the group when the wall was built.
3. All the visitors listen intently.
4. They laugh at the guide's joke.
5. An elderly man returns to the coach early.
6. The rest of the visitors climb the steep steps.

 **Punctuation**

Ending sentences

Notice that both the question mark and the exclamation mark have a built-in full stop.

Remember, a **sentence** must end with one of the following:
- a full stop (.)
- a question mark (?) if it is a question
- an exclamation mark (!) if it is an exclamation.

For example:
    I am going to visit the Great Wall of China.
    When was the Great Wall built?
    Help me, I'm falling!

A Write these sentences correctly. Don't forget the capital letters.

1 have you seen the great wall of china
2 wow, it's absolutely massive
3 when was it built
4 can it really be seen from the moon
5 that's amazing

Don't forget to begin each question with a capital letter.

B Write three questions that you might ask a guide if you were visiting the Great Wall of China.

Writing
Factual writing

All **factual writing** is true and gives the reader information. There are many different ways of presenting information. The way in which facts are written depends on their purpose.

Both pieces of writing on pages 10–11 are factual. The purpose of the Fact File is to give the reader the main, important facts about the Great Wall of China. The Fact File includes a labelled drawing to show a detail of the wall.

The purpose of the magazine article on page 10 is to encourage people to visit the Great Wall. The article includes a photograph to show readers what the Great Wall actually looks like.

A Choose one of the following subjects.
- Victoria Falls – magnificent waterfalls in Africa
- Buckingham Palace – one of the homes of the Queen
- Cheops – one of the Great Pyramids in Egypt

Research your chosen subject and make a fact file of important details about the place.

B Use the facts you researched in part A to write a report for a travel magazine. The purpose of the report is to provide information about the place in a way that will encourage readers to visit.

unit 3
Flood Disaster

The Weekly News
Saturday, 10th May

BANGLADESH DEATH TOLL REACHES 40,000

by Kareem Khan

Thousands are feared dead after the latest disaster to hit the Bay of Bengal. A cyclone and a 10 m high tidal wave surged across the coastal region of Bangladesh last Friday.

Three thousand bodies have been recovered so far, but estimates put the death toll at up to 40,000.

Communications with coastal areas and islands are not yet fully restored, but a spokesperson at the disaster relief headquarters said, "At least 7,000 people are missing from the coastal villages alone. At this stage, it is impossible to say how many people are missing from the offshore islands."

The President immediately cancelled a planned visit to Canada. He said that this was one of the worst tragedies to hit Bangladesh in the twentieth century and pledged the Government's help for the 250,000 people who have lost their homes in the flooding.

Helicopters are dropping food and drinking water to survivors, and ships from the Bangladesh navy are ploughing through heavy seas to reach the cut off islands. One report said that hundreds of survivors on bamboo rafts and floating rooftops were at risk of falling prey to sharks and crocodiles.

No one can say for certain what caused the freak wave, but people have their own opinions. Some say it was a result of global warming, while others blame underwater nuclear explosions. Other members of the community claim that humanity has incurred the wrath of the gods. Only one thing is certain — the devastation that this wave has caused is yet another burden for these impoverished, struggling people to contend with.

GLOSSARY
death toll the number of people who have died
impoverished very poor
tidal wave a huge wave
global warming an increase in the Earth's temperature
offshore at sea, some distance from the shore

Comprehension

A Copy and complete these sentences.

1 A _____ and a huge _____ _____ hit the Bay of Bengal.
2 The wave was _____ metres high.
3 At least 7,000 people are missing from _____ villages.
4 The President cancelled a visit to _____.
5 Survivors on rafts are in danger from _____ and _____.

B Find the following words in the newspaper report. Think carefully about what each means and explain it in your own words. Use a dictionary to check your answers.

1 heavy seas
2 falling prey to
3 freak wave
4 incurred the wrath
5 to contend with
6 fully restored

C Use the newspaper report to help you decide whether each sentence below is fact or opinion.

1 The death toll was 40,000.
2 The President cancelled a visit to Canada.
3 This was the worst disaster to hit Bangladesh in the twentieth century.
4 Helicopters dropped food and drinking water to survivors.
5 The disaster was caused by global warming.
6 Humanity has incurred the wrath of the gods.

Vocabulary
Synonyms

Remember, words or groups of words that mean the same, or nearly the same, are called **synonyms**. For example:

A 10 m high tidal wave <u>surged across</u> the coastal region.

Instead of 'surged across', the writer could have put 'washed over', 'flowed through' or 'rolled across'.

Newspaper reporters think carefully about synonyms to help them choose the most powerful and descriptive words and phrases.

A Find the following words in the newspaper report on page 16. Write a synonym of each word.

1 region   2 recovered   3 relief   4 cancelled
5 century 6 huge   7 disaster 8 communications

A **phrase** is a group of words.

B Here are some phrases from the report in the *Weekly News*. Write each in your own words. Use a thesaurus or dictionary to help you.

1 thousands are feared dead
2 not yet fully restored
3 ploughing through heavy seas
4 falling prey to sharks and crocodiles
5 yet another burden for these impoverished, struggling people to contend with

Spelling
Changing verb tenses

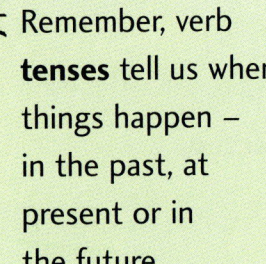
Remember, verb **tenses** tell us when things happen – in the past, at present or in the future.

To write about things that happened in the past, we usually add 'ed' or 'd' to a verb to make the **past tense**. For example:

fear   fear<u>ed</u>   restore   restore<u>d</u>

With some verbs, we don't add 'ed' or 'd' but change the middle vowel. For example:

s<u>i</u>nk   s<u>a</u>nk

With some verbs, the whole word is changed to make the past tense. For example:

speak   spoke   think   thought

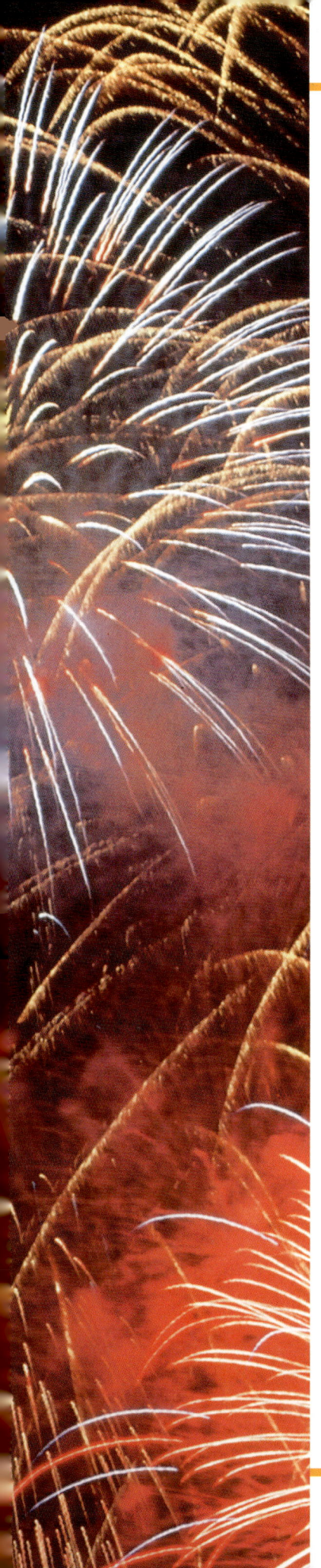

Fireworks use explosive material to make attractive and exciting displays of light, noise and smoke. Although they are thought of today as part of celebrations, they were originally used in battle. Fireworks and bonfires are fun but, every year, people are injured and even killed by accidents with fireworks. It is important to be extremely careful. On Bonfire Night, remember to follow the Firework Code.

The Firework Code

Fireworks and bonfires are fun but DANGEROUS! Be careful and always make sure an adult is with you in case of an emergency.

- Keep fireworks in a closed box.
- Take fireworks out one at a time and then close the box again.
- Read the instructions on each firework by the light of a torch.
- Light all fireworks at arm's length.
- Never return to a firework once it has been lit.
- Never throw fireworks.
- Never put fireworks in your pocket.
- Keep pets indoors.

Remember, the safest way to enjoy fireworks is at an organised display. The fireworks will be bigger and better than any you could have at home!

 **Comprehension**

B Write a sentence to answer each question about the Firework Code.
1. What will be the result if you follow these rules carefully?
2. How many rules are there?
3. Write the verb or verbs from each rule.
4. These rules tell you things that you should do and things that you shouldn't do.
    a. Which rules tell you things that you should do?
    b. Which rules tell you things that you shouldn't do?

C Do you think the instructions for building a bonfire are easy or difficult to follow? Give your reasons.

Vocabulary

Using nouns as verbs and verbs as nouns

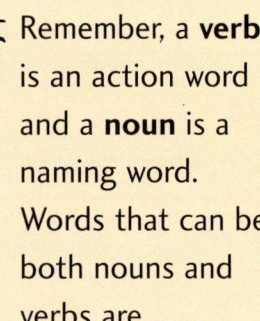

Remember, a **verb** is an action word and a **noun** is a naming word. Words that can be both nouns and verbs are **homonyms**.

We can sometimes use nouns as verbs, or verbs as nouns! For example:
Dad is going to light the fire. → **verb**

Gran turns the light off so that she can see the fireworks. → **noun**

A Write two sentences for each word, using it as a noun in the first and as a verb in the second.

1 fire   2 match   3 box   4 display

B Make a list of some other words that can be verbs or nouns.

Spelling

Homophones

Remember, **homophones** are words that sound the same but are spelt differently and have different meanings. For example:
We saw the rockets soar into the night sky.

A Copy these sentences and choose the correct words to complete them.

1 Does anyone no/know where the matches are?
2 It is good that the whether/weather has stayed dry.
3 Make sure/shore everyone stands right/write back.
4 Can you see/sea two/to read/reed the instructions?
5 Please weight/wait there/their until the fireworks are over.

B Use each pair of homophones in a sentence of your own about a firework party.

1 here   hear   2 new   knew
3 to   two   4 wear where

unit 4 Fireworks

Grammar

Verb tenses

The **present tense** can be written in two ways. For example:

Kathryn lights the fire.

or

Kathryn is lighting the fire.

'Helper' verb

Both are happening now, so both are in the present tense.

A **phrase** is a group of words.

A Write the two present-tense versions of each of these past-tense phrases. The first one has been done to help you.

1 we watched   we watch   we are watching
2 I helped
3 they built
4 she made
5 he collected
6 we checked
7 they took

B Copy the sentences below. Change them into the present tense, and write them as if they are instructions to tell someone how to make hot dogs. The first one has been done to help you.

1 We bought a sausage for each person.

Buy a sausage for each person.

2 We found an old frying pan.

3 The sausages were put in the pan with sliced onions.

4 We cooked them over the hot embers at the edge of the bonfire.

5 When they were cooked, we put the sausages into bread rolls.

Punctuation

Special uses of capital letters

An **exclamation** is when somebody says something surprising, shocking, angry or unexpected.

Remember, we use **capital letters** to begin sentences, for proper nouns and for the word 'I'. For example:

My dad says Jenny and I can go to Brentford with him to choose the fireworks.

Sometimes, we use capital letters to draw special attention to words that are very important. For example:

Fireworks and bonfires are VERY DANGEROUS!

A Copy these messages, using capital letters to begin the sentences and for the most important words in each sentence.

1. danger! always close the lid before lighting a firework.

2. keep out! these old pit workings are extremely dangerous.

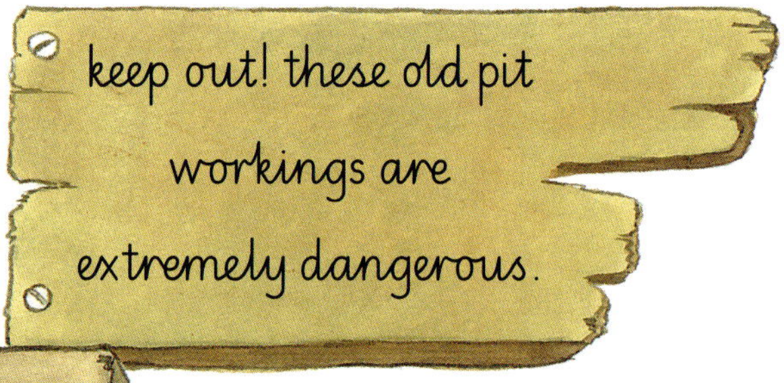

3. stop! dismount and walk across the railway crossing.

4. caution! keep out of reach of children.

5. no swimming! fast-flowing river.

B Make a sign that you could put up at your next firework party to warn everyone to keep well clear when the fireworks are being set off.

Writing

Instructions

Instructions are written for many different reasons. They may tell us how to:
- make something, for example, a bonfire
- do something safely, for example, use fireworks
- mend something, for example, a puncture
- get somewhere, for example, to find somebody's house.

Instructions have to be:
- easy to understand
- in the correct order.

Instructions are often:
- written in short sentences
- numbered
- written with a verb at the beginning, telling you what to do
- written as DOs and DON'Ts.

Write a clear set of instructions for doing one of the following.

- building a sandcastle

- travelling from your house to school
- mending a puncture

Remember to:
- give your instructions a title so the reader will know what they are for
- begin by listing the things you need, if any
- number your instructions in the correct order.

What is a Siege?

When an enemy surrounds a castle or a town, it is called a siege. Sieges have taken place throughout history – right through to modern times. In medieval times, sieges were very common.

Methods of attack

Attackers would camp outside a castle or town, preventing anyone from escaping, and stopping food and other supplies from being taken in. The siege ended when either those inside or the attackers surrendered (gave up). It could be a long wait, sometimes lasting for months or even years! During this time the attackers would often creep away and hide quietly in the woods, or march around the castle making lots of noise.

The attacking army would try to get into the castle. One way to do this was to dig a tunnel under the walls, but this could take a long time. Another way of breaking in was to use a battering ram, a huge log of wood that they pounded against the door to break it down. Huge catapults, called trebuchets, would be set up 200—300 m from the castle and used to hurl giant rocks at the walls. If there was a moat, the attackers would try to fill in part of it, so that they could get across and try to climb up the walls using ropes and ladders.

Methods of defence

Of course, people in castles knew of the many ways an enemy would try to attack, so they were usually prepared. All the land near the walls was cleared of trees and bushes. The people inside the castle would stock up with large amounts of food, so they had enough supplies to withstand a long siege.

When an attack happened, the defenders inside the castle would pull up the drawbridge and drop the portcullis across the great doorway. Soldiers would climb up onto the ramparts and fire arrows through slits in the walls. They would also pour boiling tar or heavy objects down on the attackers. Sometimes, at night, small raiding parties from inside the castle would be sent out through hidden gates in the castle walls, to take the attackers by surprise.

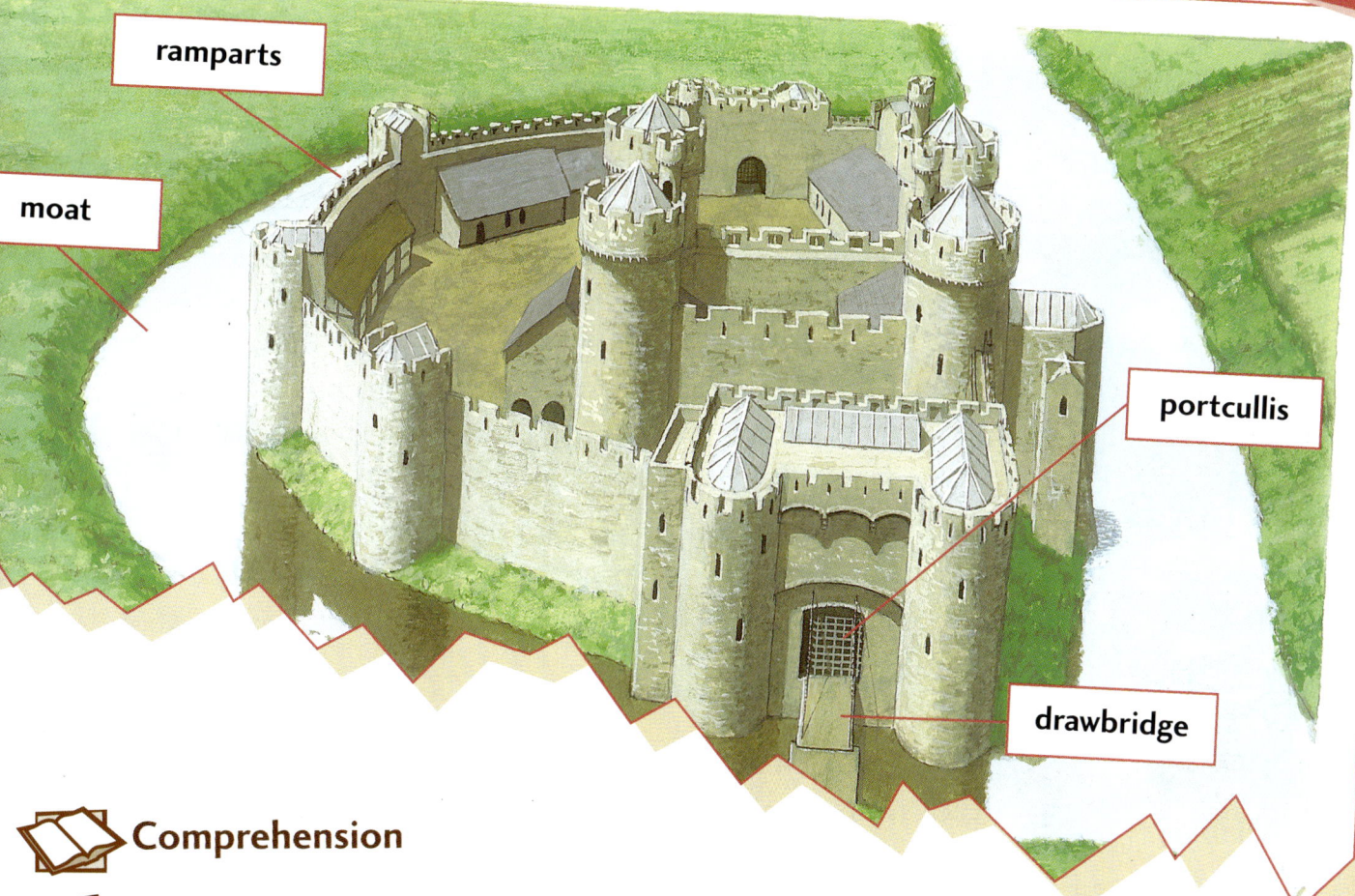

Comprehension

A Write a sentence to answer each question.
1. What is a siege?
2. Explain one way in which an attacker could get inside a castle.
3. Why would people living in a castle stock up with large amounts of food?
4. How were attackers stopped from getting inside a castle?

B Write a sentence to answer each question.
1. Suggest one reason why each side in a siege might give up.
2. Why do you think the attackers set up the trebuchet 200–300 m away from the castle walls?
3. Why might the attackers sometimes hide in the surrounding woods?
4. Why might attackers sometimes march around the castle making a noise?
5. Why do you think the land near the castle walls was kept free from trees and bushes?

C
1. How many paragraphs are there in the passage? Write a phrase or short sentence to say what each paragraph is about.
2. Copy three sentences from the passage and underline the key words.

Vocabulary

Old and new words

Many words that were used in the past are hardly ever used today, because life has changed. For example:

    drawbridge   jester   trebuchet   moat

But new words are being added to the English language all the time. Sometimes, they are invented, like the names of new machines or scientific discoveries that were not known about before. For example:

    satellite   website   digital   skateboard

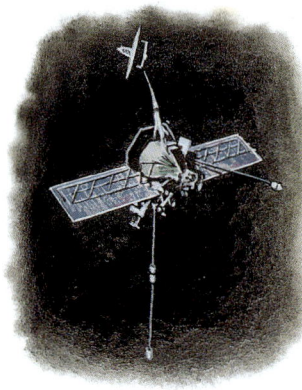

A Look at the passage on page 28. Make a list of as many modern words as possible that the people who lived in medieval times would not have known.

B Look at the passage on page 28. Make a list of as many words as possible that might have been used in medieval times but which we don't often use now.

Spelling

Syllables

In some short words, 'y' acts as a vowel, and makes a vowel sound.

Remember, a **syllable** is a part of a word that can be sounded by itself. Each syllable has its own vowel sound. For example:

    war – is pronounced as one sound, so it has one syllable
    castle – is pronounced 'ca-stle', so it has two syllables
    enemy – is pronounced 'en-em-y', so it has three syllables

A Look at the passage on page 28. Find and write down six words that have:

    1 one syllable   **2** two syllables   **3** three syllables

B Write a word that rhymes with each of the following words and has the same number of syllables. The first one has been done to help you.

    1 tunnel   *funnel*
    2 town   **3** boiling   **4** muddle   **5** trying
    6 breaking   **7** food   **8** battering   **9** moat

Grammar

Pairs of adjectives

Note the comma between each pair of adjectives.

Remember, **adjectives** tell us more about nouns. Using two or three adjectives together can make your writing more powerful. For example:

the <u>poor, starving</u> peasants

The adjectives 'poor' and 'starving' tell us different things about the peasants.

A Choose two adjectives from the box that could be used in each phrase below.

cheerful   moonlit
cold   clever
noisy   heavy
aggressive   high
cunning   stone
amusing   solid

1   the _____ , _____ court jester
2   the _____ , _____ drawbridge
3   the _____ , _____ army commander
4   the _____ , _____ castle dogs
5   the _____ , _____ ramparts
6   the _____ , _____ night

B Use each phrase you completed in part A in a sentence of your own.

Punctuation

Apostrophes for possession

To show that something belongs to a person or a thing, we add an **apostrophe** (') and an 's'. For example:
 the knight's castle = the castle belonging to the knight
 the castle's tower = the tower of the castle
These words are called **possessive nouns**.

A Write each phrase in a shorter way, using a possessive noun. The first one has been done to help you.

1. the castle belonging to the knight   the knight's castle
2. the cottage belonging to the peasant
3. the bow that belongs to the archer
4. the horse that belongs to the soldier
5. the hooves of the horse
6. the wheels of the cart
7. the sword that belongs to the knight
8. the helmet of the soldier

B Use each of these phrases in a sentence of your own.

1. the castle's drawbridge
2. the knight's armour
3. the army's flag
4. the jester's hat

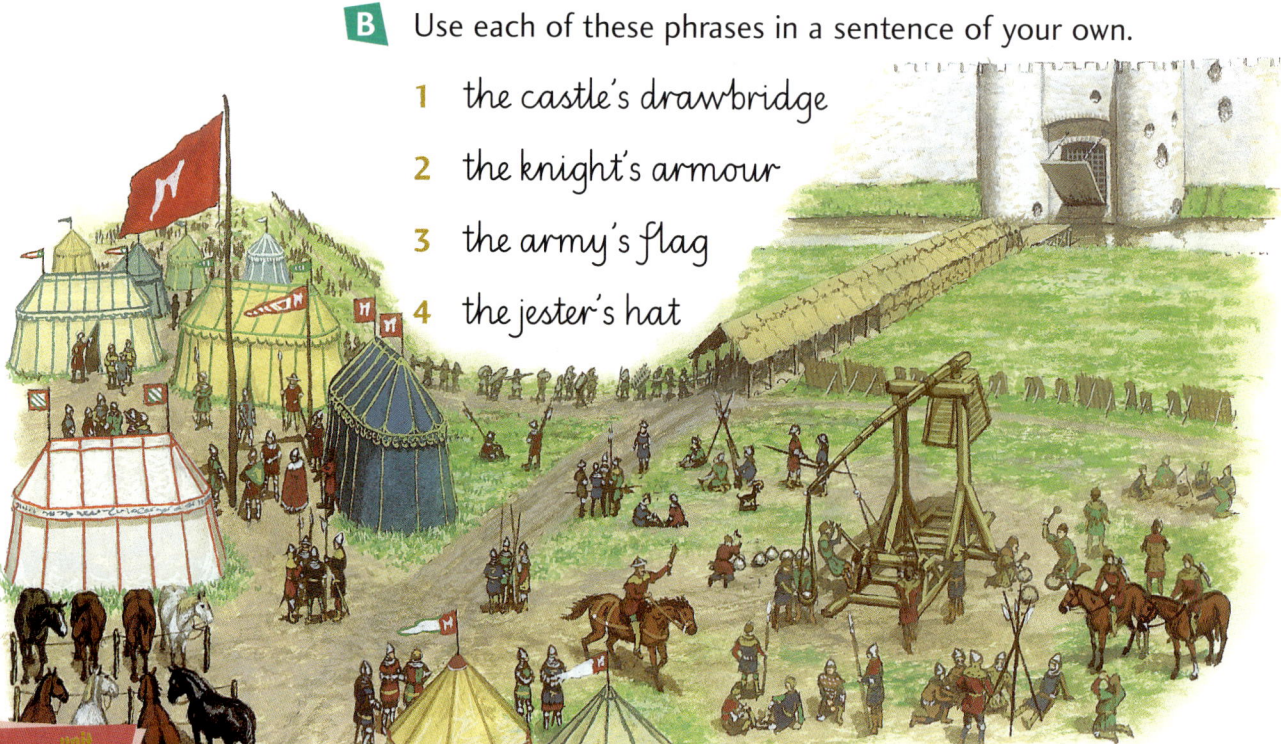

Writing

Explanations

The passage 'What is a siege?' is a piece of information text. Its purpose is to **explain** how something was done. It explains how castles and towns were attacked and defended.

This type of writing usually has an **introduction**. In the passage on page 28, the introduction is the first paragraph, which introduces what the text is about.

Information text is usually organised into **paragraphs**, with a **main heading** and **sub-headings**. This helps the reader to follow the explanation.

A **diagram** or **photograph** and its **caption** help the reader to understand more about the things mentioned in the text.

> Remember, only note down the most important words and phrases, not whole sentences.

A Read through 'What is a siege?' again. Make brief notes on the important points:

1. how castles and towns were attacked
2. how castles and towns were defended.

B Write a piece of information text about one of the following subjects.

- your school
- your favourite sport or hobby
- your pet

Organise your work by:
- making notes
- grouping your notes into paragraphs
- giving the explanation a title and dividing it into sections by using sub-headings
- including a diagram or picture and a caption.

33

Rubbish **unit 6**

Recycling

What we throw away

'Rubbish' is what we call the things we throw away because we don't want them. Rubbish can be:

- sweet wrappers
- crisp packets
- food tins
- drink cans
- food waste
- cardboard boxes
- old newspapers
- garden waste
- glass bottles and jars
- plastic food packaging
  … and lots more!

On average, each person in Britain throws away more than half a kilogram of rubbish every day.

That is about:
- 4.5 kilograms of rubbish a week
- 18 kilograms of rubbish a month
- 216 kilograms of rubbish a year
- A family of four people throws away over 800 kilograms of rubbish a year

Green Valley District Council
CONFUSED ABOUT RECYCLING?

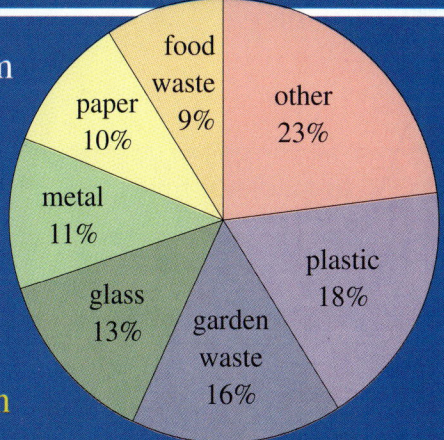

This diagram shows the composition of the rubbish collected from dustbins in the district last year:

More than half of this rubbish could have been recycled instead of going to landfill sites. Green Valley Council has started several schemes to help you to recycle more of your rubbish.

Here's how:

- All paper and glass can be taken to the special bins at collection points in the car parks in towns and villages in the area.
- All aluminium and steel cans and plastic can be placed in the special boxes provided for each household, which will be emptied when the weekly refuse collection is carried out.
- From January, you will be able to take garden waste to your local tip, where it will be shredded and made into garden compost.
- You can take rubbish of all kinds to your local tip, where about 30% of it is recycled, including metal objects, furniture, electrical items, fabric and garden waste.

For more information about recycling in the Green Valley area, contact the Council offices.

 Comprehension

A
1. Write down three examples of rubbish.
2. How much rubbish does each person in Britain throw away in a month?
3. What makes up 13% of the rubbish in the dustbins of Green Valley?
4. What are the 'special recycling bins' in Green Valley's car parks used for?

B Write a sentence to answer each question.
1. How many kilograms of rubbish does a person in Britain throw away in two weeks?
2. How many kilograms of rubbish would a family of three throw away each year?
3. What do you understand by the term 'recycling'?
4. What do you understand by the term 'landfill sites'?

C Read the information about rubbish carefully. Write at least five questions about rubbish that the passage does not answer.

Vocabulary

Over-used words – 'nice'

Like 'got', '**nice**' is one of the most over-used words in the English language. You can usually find a better word to use. For example:

The smell of the rubbish was not <u>nice</u>.

can change to: The smell of the rubbish was not <u>pleasant</u>.

or: The smell of the rubbish was <u>revolting</u>.

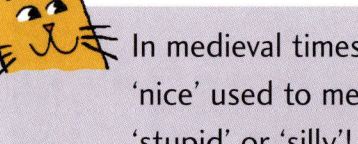

In medieval times 'nice' used to mean 'stupid' or 'silly'!

A Copy the paragraph below. Replace each 'nice' with a word from the box, or a word of your own, if you prefer.

pleasant	warm	sunny	kind	clean	fun
thoughtful	friendly	sensible	enjoyable		
relaxing	short	brief	good	helpful	tidy

It was a <u>nice</u> day. Our <u>nice</u> teacher suggested that it would be <u>nice</u> if we went outside for a <u>nice</u> break. He said it would be <u>nice</u> to make the school look <u>nice</u> by collecting the rubbish. It is not <u>nice</u> when people drop litter, but it was not <u>nice</u> for us going out to pick up their rubbish. I hope our <u>nice</u> teacher doesn't give us a <u>nice</u> treat like that again!

B Use three of the words from the box in part A and use them in sentences of your own.

Spelling

'le', 'al' and 'el' word endings

It is easy to confuse '**le**', '**al**' and '**el**' endings because they all sound similar! For example:

recyc<u>le</u>   met<u>al</u>   barr<u>el</u>

A Many words that end in 'al' are adjectives. Make an adjective that ends with 'al' from each of these nouns.

1 medicine   2 fact   3 accident   4 history

5 music   6 centre   7 nation   8 addition

B 1 Sort these words into three sets, according to their endings.

| rubble | grovel | shovel | local | crumble |
| tropical | novel | humble | hovel | mechanical |

2 Some verbs end in 'le'. Add 'ing' and then 'ed' to make the present tense and then the past tense of each verb.

a paddle   b handle   c dangle   d twinkle

e rustle   f jostle   g grumble   h tumble

3 Write a rule about what happens when you add 'ing' to a verb that ends with 'le'.

Grammar

Adjective phrases

An adjective phrase often comes after the noun it describes.

Remember, sometimes you need to use an **adjective phrase** when a single adjective is not enough to describe a noun. For example:
   The rubbish, smelly and rat-infested, urgently needed to be buried.

The adjective phrase 'smelly and rat-infested' describes 'rubbish' (a noun) and so acts as an adjective. Adjective phrases make your writing more interesting.

Notice that the sentence still makes sense without the adjective phrase – 'The rubbish urgently needed to be buried.'

A Copy each sentence and fill the gap with an adjective phrase from the box below.

1 The tins and cans, _____, are sold for recycling.

2 The new-style bins, _____, make the refuse collectors' work much easier.

3 The refuse lorry, _____, struggled up the hill.

| with a full load of rubbish aboard |
| larger and with sturdy wheels |
| some steel and some aluminium |

B Write three sentences about how and why we need to protect our environment. Use an adjective phrase in each one and underline it.

Punctuation

Apostrophes for possession

Remember, to show that something belongs to someone or something (ownership), we add an **apostrophe** (') and an 's'. For example:
   The dustbin's lid fell off.   (the lid belongs to the dustbin)

For plural nouns, which usually end in 's' already – like 'dustbins' – we simply put an apostrophe after the 's'.
For example:
   The three dustbins' lids fell off.

For nouns that are plural, but don't end with 's' – like 'men' – we add 's.
For example:
   The three men's hats fell off.

Remember, adding an apostrophe or 's to a noun to show ownership makes it into a **possessive noun**.

A Rewrite each phrase correctly, adding an apostrophe to each purple word to show ownership.

1 the birds nests
2 the womans coat
3 the womens overalls
4 the rats tails
5 ten mens gloves
6 the childrens games
7 a clowns hat
8 the lorrys wheels

Remember to check whether the noun is singular or plural.

B Rewrite these phrases in a shorter way, using possessive nouns.

1 the tools belonging to the workmen
2 the lid of the dustbin
3 waste food from the restaurant
4 the car park in the town
5 rubbish from the two factories

Suspension Bridges

Rose Steel

In 1826, Thomas Telford completed the 177 metre long Menai suspension bridge, which was supported by cables of wrought-iron links. It carried two lanes of roadway traffic over the straits.

Many of the longest modern road bridges over rivers are suspension bridges. They are made from steel cables. Two large towers are built and the steel cables are hung between them. More cables hang down from the main cables and these 'suspend' the road. This is why these bridges are called 'suspension' bridges. The road is high enough for ships to pass underneath.

The Forth, Severn and Humber Bridges are examples of suspension bridges in Britain. When it was opened, in 1981, the Humber Bridge had the longest span of any bridge in the world. Its main span is 1,410 metres across.

The Forth Road Bridge, Scotland

Comprehension

A
1. Which book gives you information on early bridges?
2. In which book would you find information about the Menai suspension bridge?
3. In which book would you find information about the Tacoma Narrows bridge?
4. Find and copy the names of three suspension bridges.
5. What aspect of bridges has O. Dear written about?

B Explain in your own words what you understand by the phrase in blue in each sentence below.

1. It carried two lanes of roadway traffic over the straits.
2. The Humber Bridge had the longest span of any bridge in the world.
3. Over the years, many bridges have collapsed, mostly during construction.

C Choose one of the three passages about bridges. Make notes on the passage by writing down key words and phrases.

Vocabulary

Definitions

'Bridge' has four different meanings. Remember, words like this are called homonyms.

These are the dictionary definitions for the word 'bridge':

bridge 1 *n* a passageway across a river or other barrier 2 *n* the captain's platform over a ship's deck 3 *n* a card game like whist 4 *v* to link two things

n = noun
v = verb

A 1 Without using a dictionary, write a definition for each word below, using no more than seven words. Some of the words have more than one meaning. Use seven words to explain each meaning of each word.

    a stream   **b** creeper   **c** trunk
    d steel   **e** suspend   **f** beam

2 Now write a definition for the words in question 1, but use only four words for each definition.

3 Check your definitions in a dictionary.

B Use each word below in a sentence of your own. Write a separate sentence for each meaning of the word.

  1 bridge   **2** trunk   **3** beam

Spelling

Using a dictionary

Remember, it is easy to find a word in your **dictionary** because the words are organised in **alphabetical order**. When sorting words into alphabetical order, you need to look at the first letter of each word. If the first letters are the same, you need to look at the second letter, and so on.

bri**c**k   bri**d**ge   bri**g**ht   bri**l**liant   bris**t**le

a b c d e f g h i j k l m n o p q r s t u v w x y z

rain**b**ow   rain**c**oat   rain**d**rop   rain**f**all   rain**w**ear

unit 7 Bridges

42

A Sort these words into alphabetical order.

1. lorry   bus   visit   journey   street   water
2. time   tower   coach   ticket   crash   car
3. ridge   road   river   railway   rock   race
4. bridge   break   brick   build   brake   bunker
5. travel   truck   train   tram   tarmac   track

B Use a dictionary to help you check the spelling of these words, then write them correctly.

1. scisors   2. adress   3. becuse   4. colapse
5. ocassion   6. alltogether   7. recieve   8. peices

Grammar
Adjectives

Remember, an **adjective** is a describing word. We use a **comparative adjective** to describe the difference between <u>two</u> things. To make a comparative adjective, you usually need to add 'er'. But, if the original adjective ends in 'y', you must drop the 'y' and add 'ier'. For example:
  long   long<u>er</u>   silly   sill<u>ier</u>

We use a **superlative adjective** to describe the difference between <u>three or more</u> things. To make a superlative adjective, you usually need to add 'est'. But, if the original adjective ends in 'y', you must drop the 'y' and add 'iest'. For example:
  long   long<u>est</u>   silly   sill<u>iest</u>

A Choose an adjective to complete each sentence.

1. The Forth Railway bridge is <u>old/older/oldest</u> than the Forth Road bridge.
2. The <u>busy/busier/busiest</u> time for traffic on the bridge is between 5 p.m. and 6 p.m.
3. When it was opened, the Humber Bridge was the <u>long/longer/longest</u> suspension bridge in the world.

Be careful! Some words end with 'y'.

B Copy and complete the table below.

Adjective	Comparative adjective	Superlative adjective
small	smaller	smallest
slow		
high		
short		
happy		
funny		

 **Sentence construction**

Word order

Remember, the meaning of a **sentence** depends not just on the words you use but the order in which you use them. **Phrases** need to be in the correct position, as near as possible to the words they relate to most closely. For example:

We saw some red poppies walking around the field.

The poppies weren't really walking around the field! A much better way to write the sentence would be:

Walking around the field, we saw some red poppies.

A Rewrite these sentences, putting the phrases in a better order.

1. I saw a stray dog waiting for a bus to arrive.
2. I saw the birds near the flowers that were twittering.
3. The teacher punished the boys who had talked during the lesson after school.
4. The farmer milked the cows wearing rubber overalls.

B Make up two sentences of your own that can have different, and funny, meanings if the phrases are in the wrong order.

Writing

Collecting information

When you are writing a piece of **information** text, your 'sources' are the places where you get your information, such as books, magazines, computer software or the Internet.

Different sources will give you different information about a subject. The passages on pages 40 and 41 come from three books. The books provide information on:

- the earliest bridges
- bridge disasters
- suspension bridges.

When you find information in sources, you need to make notes by writing down the key words and phrases.

If you were looking for information on what bridges are made of, your notes might look like this:

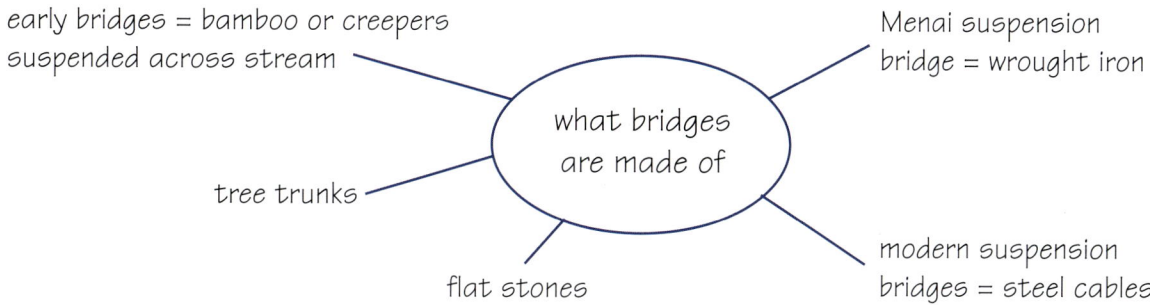

A Read the passages on pages 40 and 41.

1. Make notes on suspension bridges. Remember that your notes should be key words and phrases, not whole sentences.
2. Use your notes to write a short passage about suspension bridges.

B Look at the drawing of a tree-trunk bridge below:

The notes around the drawing are called **annotations**.

Draw either a clapper bridge or an early suspension bridge. Draw lines to the various part of your sketch and add annotations that will help the reader to understand the picture.

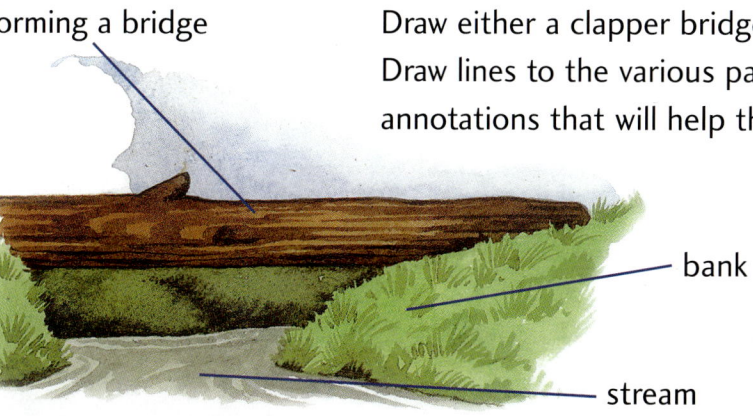

Unit 8 Snow stories — Footprints

Notes for report about strange happening in Devon

1854–55: cold winter according to Met. Office

Feb. night – snow – Devon

Next morning – footprints – miles

footprints – 4 inches (10 cm)
two legs
hooves

footprints began Totnes, ended Littleham near Dawlish, footprints went through wood – dogs wouldn't go in wood

Sir Richard Owen, studies animals – badger

Rev Henry Fusden – lots of cats

opinions

Local people – the devil

Other opinions – fox, donkey, otter, kangaroo

N.B. explain 'Met. Office'

Comprehension

A
1. In what month did this strange happening take place?
2. Where did the footprints begin?
3. Where did the footprints end?
4. What did Sir Richard Owen think had made the footprints?
5. What did the local people think had made the footprints?

Report on strange incident of February 1855

According to the Met. Office, the winter of 1854 to 1855 was very cold, especially in the south of England. One night in February, there was a heavy fall of snow in Devon and the next morning there was a line of footprints in the snow that went on for miles. They were four inches (10 cm) long and looked as if they had been made by something with two legs and hooves.

The footprints started in a garden in Totnes, stopped in a place called Littleham, then reappeared near a village called Dawlish and went through a wood. Dogs were brought to the wood to see if they could catch what had made the footprints, but they barked and howled and would not go into the wood.

There were many different opinions about what had made the footprints. Sir Richard Owen, a man who studied animals, said that they were made by a badger. Other people said it was a fox, an otter, a donkey and even a kangaroo! The Reverend Henry Fusden said the prints were made by lots of cats. The people who lived in that part of Devon had their own opinion. They were sure that the footprints were made by the devil!

GLOSSARY

Met. Office means the Meteorological Office, an organisation for the study and forecasting of the weather

Comprehension

B 1 Find and copy the phrase which tells you it had snowed a lot.
2 Explain what the footprints looked like.
3 Do you think the footprints were made by an ordinary animal? Give your reasons.
4 Why do you think that the dogs would not go into the wood?

C 1 What is the main subject of each of the three paragraphs?
2 Write some sentences to explain what you think might have made the strange footprints.

47

Vocabulary

Making adjectives

Remember, some nouns and verbs can be turned into **adjectives** when 'y' is added. For example:

ice → icy (noun → adjective)

bounce → bouncy (verb → adjective)

There are other **suffixes** that can be used to make verbs or nouns into adjectives. For example:

drink	drink**able**
fear	fear**ful**
frighten	frighten**ing**

A Choose a suffix from the box to convert each word below into an adjective, then use it to describe a noun in a sentence of your own. The first one has been done to help you.

| able | ing | ful | worthy | ic |

1. sea — seaworthy — The leaky boat wasn't seaworthy.
2. tear
3. artist
4. sale
5. hero
6. shock
7. road
8. shame
9. love

B Draw a table like the one below. Complete it by adding ten nouns or verbs that can be made into adjectives by adding a suffix.

noun or verb	adjective	suffix
help	helpful	ful

Spelling

'dge' letter pattern

'**dge**' is a common letter pattern that makes a 'j' sound. It often comes at the end of a word. The 'dge' letter pattern can be tricky to spell because it sounds the same as the 'ge' letter pattern. For example:

ba**dg**er   ima**g**e

ju**dg**e   ra**g**e

Snow stories — unit 8

A Write down the headings 'dge' and 'ge'. Write each word from the box under the correct heading.

| badge | garage | lodger | porridge | package | damage |
| hedge | garbage | trudge | advantage | fudge | |

B Draw a table like the one below, and write as many words as you can in each section.

'adge' words	'edge' words	'idge' words	'odge' words	'udge' words
badge	edge	ridge	lodge	fudge

Grammar

Adverbs

Remember, **adverbs** tell us more about verbs. They can also tell us more about **adjectives** by varying the meaning of the adjective in a sentence. For example, 'scared' is an adjective. The adverbs 'slightly' and 'extremely' can vary its meaning:

I was <u>slightly</u> **scared**.
I was <u>extremely</u> **scared**.

Remember, many adverbs end in 'ly'.

A Write down three adverbs you could use with each adjective.

1 snowy   quite snowy   incredibly snowy
2 strange   3 heavy   4 frightening

Some adjectives don't work with most adverbs. For example:
    alive   red
Something cannot be 'very alive' or 'slightly alive'!

B Write down two other adjectives that don't work with most adverbs.

49

Sentence construction

Clauses and phrases

Conjunctions can link sentences, clauses or words.

Remember, a **clause** is a group of words that has a verb. A sentence can have one, two, three or more clauses and/or phrases. The clauses and phrases in a sentence are linked by **commas** or **conjunctions**. For example, these four clauses are linked by a comma and two conjunctions:

The footprints started in a garden in Totnes, stopped in a place called Littleham **then** reappeared near a village called Dawlish **and** went through a wood.

(comma, conjunction, conjunction)

A Choosing conjunctions from the box, add two different second clauses or phrases to each of the clauses below.

> and   so   although   because   after   when   but

1 There was a thick covering of snow
2 One man said they were badger tracks
3 Some local people thought they knew the answer

B Use conjunctions and commas to join each set of clauses to make a single sentence.

1 it had been a very cold winter
  there had been a lot of snow

2 there was a smooth covering of snow
  lying thickly over the countryside
  the strange footprints were very clear

3 they followed the tracks
  recorded their size and shape
  tried to capture the beast that had made them

Snow stories — unit 8

Writing

Fact and opinion

You can find information about a subject from different sources. Some of the information you find will be **facts**. Facts are things which are true and can be proved. For example, it is a fact that, in the south of England, the winter of 1854–55 was very cold. Another fact is that the strange footprints began in a garden in Totnes.

Some of the information you find will be **opinion**. Opinions are people's ideas and beliefs about things. For example, it was the opinion of some people that the footprints were made by the devil.

A Write the headings 'Fact' and 'Opinion' into your book. Read the passage on page 47 and write three facts and three opinions under the headings you have written.

B Here are some notes about Sir Robert Scott, an explorer who journeyed to the South Pole.

Use the notes about Sir Robert Scott to write three brief paragraphs:
- In the first paragraph, introduce who you are writing about.
- In the second paragraph, write about his first journey.
- In the third paragraph, write about his second journey.

Sir Robert Falcon Scott – born 1869, died 1912
Made two journeys to Antarctica:

(1) 1900–1904
ship called the Discovery
didn't reach the South Pole

(2) 1910–1912
ship called Terra Nova
reached South Pole on 17th Jan. 1912
another explorer – Amundsen – had already reached there on 14th Dec. 1911
Scott died on return journey

Unit 9 Roald Dahl

A Famous Author

Roald Dahl (1916–90) was one of this century's most successful writers, for both children and adults. Here is an extract from a biography of Roald Dahl, written by Chris Powling.

A **biography** is a book that somebody writes about another person's life or work.

First he would settle down in an old, battered armchair with a wooden board propped across it. Then he would sharpen six yellow pencils. Gradually, hour by hour, he would wear these out writing on a pad of yellow paper. "One of the nice things about being a writer," he once said, "is that all you need is what you've got in your head and a pencil and a bit of paper."

What Roald Dahl had in his head was *The Twits*, and *George's Marvellous Medicine* and *Esio Trot* and *The Minpins*, as well as *The Giraffe and the Pelly and Me*. Slowly, steadily, Roald Dahl's books made him one of the richest and most famous writers for children there has ever been.

Of course, that does not mean life was always easy. Plenty of grown-ups did not like his writing at all – and still don't. "He's too rude," they complain. "He only appeals to the bad side of children. His stories won't make them better people."

You must make up your own mind about that.

Comprehension

A 1 What does 'battered' tell you about the armchair?
2 Why do you think Roald Dahl needed six pencils at a time?
3 What did Roald Dahl mean when he said that, to be a writer, "all you need is what you've got in your head and a pencil and a bit of paper"?
4 Write down the titles of two of Roald Dahl's books.
5 What are the three reasons why some grown-ups do not like Dahl's books?

8 Grass Hill
Blotwich
BW21 6SN
23rd May

Dear Mrs Frost,

I am writing to you regarding the book you are reading with my son's class.

I feel that 'James and the Giant Peach' is not suitable reading material for eight-year-olds. My son is enjoying the story but children will enjoy many things that we, as adults, should steer them away from.

Quite frankly, Dahl seems to have only two things in mind – to make adults look stupid and to give children many bad and wrong ideas!

Surely, we should be guiding children's reading and not be content just to give them books they will find amusing because it makes life easier.

I hope you will not be reading Dahl's books to your class in the future!

Yours sincerely,

Gordon Bothersome

Comprehension

 1 How many paragraphs does the letter have?

 2 Copy and complete this table summarising what is in each paragraph.

Paragraph 1	says why he is writing
Paragraph 2	
Paragraph 3	
Paragraph 4	
Paragraph 5	

 1 The biography extract is an information passage. Write two or three sentences to say what it is informing you about.

2 The letter is an example of persuasive writing. Write two or three paragraphs to say what it is trying to persuade Mrs Frost to do.

Vocabulary

Using a thesaurus

Remember, a **thesaurus** is a book that gives the synonyms and the antonym (if it has one) of many common words. It may also list other words from the same word family.

Remember, **synonyms** are words that mean the same, or nearly the same.
Antonyms are words that mean the opposite.

A

1. Find the following words in the letter from Mr Bothersome. Use a thesaurus to find some other words that he could have used instead.
   - a steer
   - b stupid
   - c suitable
   - d content

2. Now write the antonym (if it has one) of each word from question 1.

3. Copy each sentence, using a thesaurus to help you choose the best synonym to replace each pink word.

   a "I think Roald Dahl's books are exciting," said Mrs Frost.

   b "Maybe," replied Mr Bothersome, "but standards will fall if children read such nonsense."

   c "I want to teach the children to enjoy reading," snapped Mrs Frost.

You may have to remove or change other words to make the sentences mean the opposite.

B Use a thesaurus to find the antonyms of the pink words. Then use them to write each sentence so it has the opposite meaning.

1. "I disagree with you about Roald Dahl," said Mr Bothersome.

2. "I think he is a superb writer," cried Mrs Frost.

3. "Many experts praise his writing," she added.

4. "My son's behaviour will get worse if he continues reading Dahl," insisted Mr Bothersome.

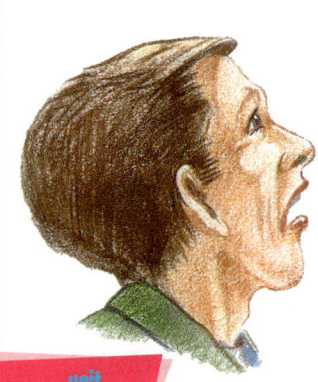

Spelling

Root words

Remember, many words are made of several parts, including a **root** with a prefix and/or a suffix. For example:

'biography' is made from bio + graph + y

'bio' means life and 'graph' means writing, so, biography means a written account of somebody's life

Words in the same word family share the same root. For example, these words have the root 'graph':

auto<u>graph</u>   para<u>graph</u>   geo<u>graph</u>y   photo<u>graph</u>   autobio<u>graph</u>y

A Use a dictionary to find the definition of each word.

1. a autograph   b paragraph   c autobiography
2. What does the root 'graph' mean?

B Be a dictionary detective!

1. Copy each group of words. Underline the root of each group and write a definition of it.

   a physical   physician   physiotherapy   physique

   b atmosphere   hemisphere   spherical   biosphere

   c microphone   telephone   saxophone   phonics

In some words, the root word may not be complete.

2. a What do all the words in question 1 have in common?
   b From what language do we get this letter pattern?
   c Write down six other words that include this letter pattern.

Grammar

Adjectives and adverbs

Remember, an adjective describes a noun, and an adverb describes a verb.

Remember, **adjectives** can be used to compare two things by adding the suffix 'er' or the word 'more'. They can be used to compare three or more things by adding the suffix 'est' or the word 'most'. For example:

| warm | warm<u>er</u> | warm<u>est</u> |
| dangerous | <u>more</u> dangerous | <u>most</u> dangerous |

Some **adverbs** can be used in a similar way to compare two or more <u>actions</u>. For example:

I arrived <u>late</u>. The children ran <u>quickly</u>.
I arrived <u>later</u> than you. Joe ran <u>more quickly</u> than Sam.
I arrived <u>latest</u>. Thomas ran <u>most quickly</u>.

Many adverbs are also adjectives. For example:

John caught the <u>early</u> train.   John left <u>early</u> for work.

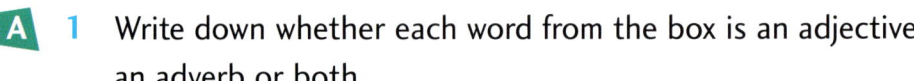

A 1 Write down whether each word from the box is an adjective, an adverb or both.

> tall small late large fast funny
> terrible high far beautiful unkind hard

2 Draw a table like the one below, and complete it, using all the words from part A.

	+ 'er' or 'more'	+ 'est' or 'most'
tall	taller	tallest

B 1 Write whether the pink word or words are adjectives or adverbs.

a Please laugh more quietly as you read that book!

b The BFG is the most enjoyable book I've ever read.

c Roald Dahl is one of the greatest children's writers.

2. Use each adverb from part A, question 1 as an adjective in a sentence of your own.

Sentence construction

Setting out a letter

A. Imagine you are going to write a letter to a relative or a friend. Set out the top of the letter, with your home address, the date and the name of the person you are writing to.

B. Imagine you are going to write a letter to your favourite author, asking him/her to come to your school and talk to your class. Set out the top of the letter, with your school's address, the date and the name of the author.

Writing

Writing to persuade

The purpose of some types of writing is to **persuade** the reader to do something or to believe something. Advertisements, posters, television and radio commercials and brochures all try to persuade us to buy things, visit places, see films, vote for a political party, etc.

In Mr Bothersome's letter, he tried to persuade Mrs Frost to stop reading Roald Dahl's books with the children in her class.

When you write a persuasive letter to put your point of view about something, you should:

- begin by saying why you are writing
- explain the reasons why you think your point of view is reasonable
- make it clear at the end what you would like the person receiving the letter to do and whether you expect a reply.

A. Imagine you are Mrs Frost and you have received the letter from Mr Bothersome. You do not agree with his point of view and think Roald Dahl is an excellent author for children to read. Write a reply to Mr Bothersome, clearly stating your point of view and giving your reasons.

B. Choose an author whose books you like to read. Write a letter to your teacher to persuade him/her to read the books in class.

Fire unit 10

Fire Beneath our Feet

Deep in the centre of the Earth, the rocks are not cold and hard, but extremely hot, which makes them **molten** like thick syrup. This hot rock is called **magma**.

Sometimes, magma forces its way up through cracks in the Earth's crust (outer layer). Magma is called **lava** once it is on the surface. The lava gushes out, along with ash and gases, in a fiery mass. The places on the Earth's surface where these eruptions occur are called **volcanoes**.

As the lava flows down the sides of the volcano, it cools and hardens. Layers of rock build up and the volcano becomes tall, with steep sides. Eventually, cooled lava blocks the opening of the volcano, like a cork in a bottle. This is called a **plug**. Soon, the volcano becomes quiet. However, old, quiet volcanoes sometimes unexpectedly erupt into life again, as magma forces out the plug.

Volcanoes that may erupt again are **active**. There are no active volcanoes in Britain, but there are some **extinct** ones. Extinct volcanoes are so old that the magma has stopped trying to force a way to the surface at this point, so we know they will never erupt again. A famous extinct volcano is the hill in Edinburgh called Arthur's Seat.

Comprehension

A Copy and complete these sentences.

1. Deep in the Earth, the rocks are very _____.
2. This hot rock is called _____.
3. _____ are formed when the lava and ash escape at the surface.
4. The famous volcano in Edinburgh is called _____.

B Write a sentence to answer each question.
1. Why are the rocks in the centre of the Earth 'like thick syrup'?
2. When does magma become known as lava?
3. Why is the plug described as being 'like a cork in a bottle'? Do you think this is a good way to describe it?
4. What is an extinct volcano?

C
1. How many paragraphs are there in the passage?
2. Make brief notes on what each paragraph is about. Remember to write down only the key words and phrases.

Vocabulary
Synonyms

Remember, **synonyms** are words or phrases with similar meanings. For example:
   'pull' and 'tug' are synonyms

Synonyms can be short phrases, too. For example:
   'burst out' and 'erupt' are synonyms

A Choose from the box a synonym of each word below.

1 molten   melted solid thick heavy
2 centre   circle middle edge corner
3 extinct   fast find gentle dead
4 extremely   very usually tiny slow

B Use a thesaurus to find at least three synonyms for each word below. Choose one of the synonyms for each word and put it into a sentence of your own.

1 quiet   2 hard   3 awful   4 damage

Spelling
it's or its?

Apostrophes are used in **contractions**. For example:
   <u>Don't</u> get too close!

Apostrophes are also used in **possessive nouns**, to show who or what owns something. For example:
   The <u>Earth's</u> molten centre is extremely hot.

The word **it's** is a contraction of 'it is' and 'it has'. For example:
   It is: <u>It's</u> very dangerous.
The apostrophe goes in place of the 'i' of 'is'.
   It has: <u>It's</u> been extinct for a long time.
The apostrophe goes in place of the 'ha' of 'has'.

Its is a **possessive pronoun**. It <u>doesn't</u> have an apostrophe. For example:
   <u>Its</u> molten centre is extremely hot.

A good way to remember this is to think that other possessive pronouns – his, hers, our, mine, your, their – don't have apostrophes either.

A Copy the sentence and fill each gap with **it's** or **its**.

1 _____ an amazing spectacle.

2 _____ crater is glowing with molten lava.

3 I can't believe _____ happening.

4 _____ effect on the countryside was terrible.

B Use both **its** and **it's** in one sentence of your own.

Grammar

Nouns and verbs

Remember, words that are spelled the same and sound the same but have different meanings are called **homonyms**.

Remember, most **nouns** are made plural by adding 's' or 'es'. For example:

singular	plural
cloud	clouds
volcano	volcanoes

However, we add 's' or 'es' to many **verbs** if they are to go with a singular noun. For example:

singular	plural
Robert sits	The boys sit
The frog jumps	The frogs jump

Remember, some words are both a noun and a verb. For example:
Noun: I made a wish when I blew out the candles.
Verb: I will wish for a bicycle.

A Write the headings 'Noun', 'Verb' and 'Both noun and verb'. Write each word from the box under the correct heading. Beside each noun, write its plural.

> fix crack rock bush wish erupt baby
> watch house vanish explode fox escape
> destroy burn burst lorry punish

B Choose four words from the list called 'Both noun and verb' that you wrote in part A. Use each word in two sentences, one as a verb and one as a noun. If you like, you could add the suffix 'ing' or 'ed' to alter the tense of the verb.

Punctuation

Punctuating sentences

A Copy these sentences, adding the missing capital letters, commas, full stops, apostrophes, question marks and exclamation marks.

1 have you ever been to edinburgh and seen arthurs seat
2 there are several active volcanoes in iceland
3 ouch that was hot
4 the lava molten hot and unstoppable soon engulfed the houses
5 it was the volcanos final devastating eruption that caused the worst damage

 Speech marks are also called **inverted commas**.

B Copy these sentences, adding the missing speech marks and commas. Remember, only the words actually spoken should be inside the speech marks. The first one has been done to help you.

1 It erupted last year warned our guide.
   "It erupted last year," warned our guide.
2 Please keep behind this wall he added as it's not safe to go any closer.
3 You may find it a steep climb up he said. However, it's an easy walk down.
4 Tom was scared. I don't like being this close to an active volcano he muttered.

 Writing

Summaries

A **summary** is a shortened version of something, which includes all the main points. To write a summary, you need to:
- understand what you have read
- write the main points in your own words.

1. Make a summary of the passage on page 58. You need to look at each paragraph in turn and write down the main points in note form. Here are notes on the first two paragraphs:

   > Paragraph 1: centre of the Earth – rocks not cold and hard rocks = hot and molten – called magma
   >
   > Paragraph 2: magma comes through cracks – now called lava – brings ash and gases

   Now make notes like these on paragraphs 3 and 4.

2. When you have made notes, you need to write the first draft of your summary, using your own words whenever possible. You can use the same number of paragraphs as the passage but they should be shorter. Here is a first draft of the summary for paragraphs 1 and 2:

   > At the centre of the Earth the rocks are not hard and cold. They are very hot and molten and are known as magma. When magma comes through the cracks in the Earth it is known as lava. It brings with it ash and gases.

   Now use your notes to write the first draft of a summary of paragraphs 3 and 4.

3. After writing a first draft, you should check that you have:
   - included all the main points
   - used your own words whenever possible
   - used correct spelling, grammar and punctuation
   - made your summary shorter than the passage.

   Check your summary and make any changes you need.

4. Neatly copy your summary.

Unit 11 India: Holidays in India

Throughout our daily lives, we are bombarded by advertisements – on television and radio, on posters, in newspapers and magazines and on the Internet. Everywhere, we are faced with words and pictures that are trying to persuade us to buy things, join things or visit places. This is an advertisement on the Internet.

India will set your pulse racing

It's exciting, exotic and entertaining. India is a blaze of colour, a clamour of noise – it will dazzle all your senses. There are ancient temples, fabulous palaces, bustling markets and tropical forests. India is a land of infinite variety, of teeming cities and peaceful villages, wild countryside and beautiful beaches. You can see the Taj Mahal at sunset, ride on the back of an elephant to the Amber Fort, taste food as varied as the country itself and view some of the world's most exotic and beautiful wildlife. We will show you the real India. You will be thrilled, fascinated, occasionally shocked – but never bored. And you'll leave India vowing to return!

Comprehension

A
1. What is this an advertisement for?
2. Who do you think the advertisement is aimed at?
3. Find and copy three phrases which are used to persuade you that this is a place you should visit.
4. Find three adjectives beginning with the letter 'e' which describe India.

India — a holiday in Paradise

Beaches so clean a turtle could eat his dinner off them. Seas as clear as glass, where the only oil pollution comes from the occasional coconut that rolls into the surf. Beaches of beautiful white coral sand that stretch for miles, edged by thickets of shady palm.

Visit India for the holiday of a lifetime

Comprehension

B
1. What particular part of India is being advertised?
2. Who do you think the advertisement is aimed at?
3. Find and copy three phrases which are used to persuade you that this is a place you must visit.

C One or both of the adverts have been successful if, after reading them, you want to visit India. If you do not want to visit India, then both of the adverts have been unsuccessful. Write down whether you would like to visit India. Give your reasons, saying why you found each advert persuasive/not persuasive.

Vocabulary
Similes

A **simile** describes something by comparing it to something else.
A simile almost always includes the words 'as' or 'like'. For example:
  Seas **as** clear **as** glass…
  The water sparkled **like** a jewel.
You can use similes in your writing to create striking pictures with words.

A Choose the best word to complete each simile, or use a word of your own if you have thought of a better one.

1 as dry as a field/desert/town/rock
2 as white as porridge/custard/snow/ink
3 as cold as ice/water/fire/milk

Remember to use 'like' or 'as' in each simile.

B Write a sentence containing a simile about each of the following. Underline the simile in each sentence.

1 a crowded Indian market
2 the colourful fruit and vegetables on the market stalls
3 a beautiful palace

Spelling
Suffix 'ion'

A very common **suffix** is 'ion'. It is added to many root words. The suffix 'ion' always has either a 't' or an 's' in front of it. For example:
  percus**s**ion   loca**t**ion
'Fashion' is the only exception to this rule, as it has 'sh' in front of the suffix 'ion'.

Remember, **root words** are words to which suffixes or prefixes are added to make other words in the same word family.

A 1 Make a word by adding the suffix 'ion' to each of these verbs. You may need to alter some words before you add the suffix.

a situate   b imitate   c prepare   d observe
e inspire   f express   g supervise h exclaim

2 Write the root word from which each of these 'ion' words was made.

a action   b demonstration   c discussion
d pollution   e reception   f opposition

B Complete the 'ion' word to fill each gap. Use a dictionary to check the correct spelling of each word you make.

1 An op_____ is carried out by a surgeon.
2 A member of your family is your rel_____.
3 Studying for exams is called rev_____.
4 Our eyesight is also called our vi_____.

Grammar

Future-tense verbs

To write about something that is going to happen in the future, we write in the **future tense**. The future tense of a verb often includes a being or helper verb. For example:

You will see the temples and palaces.

helper verb — will
main verb — see

We usually write 'shall' after 'I' and 'we', and 'will' after 'you', 'they', 'he', 'she' or 'it'. For example:

I shall visit India this year.
You will come with me.

To make a very strong statement, reverse the rule and use 'will' after 'I' and 'we', and 'shall' after 'you', 'they', 'he', 'she' or 'it'. For example:

I will go to India, whatever you say!
You shall not stop me!

A Copy the sentences, filling each gap with 'will' or 'shall'.

1 I _____ take you to the palace.
2 We _____ see beautiful sights.
3 I'm sure you _____ be impressed.
4 Alan has said he _____ bring his camera.

B Make these statements stronger.

1 You will go to bed when I say.
2 I shall do it.
3 We shall be late.
4 You will eat it.

 **Sentence construction**

Positive and negative sentences

A **positive** sentence is saying 'yes', that something can or will be done. For example:

  I would like to visit India.

A **negative** sentence is saying 'no', that something can't or won't be done. For example:

  I would not like to visit India.

A 1 Write the words from the box in two lists – 'positive words' and 'negative words'.

> do couldn't none did have didn't never yes no shouldn't can won't should wouldn't will not could haven't don't would shan't nothing shall can't always

2 What do you notice about the negative words?

B 1 Use some of the words from the box in part A to help you to write these positive sentences as negative sentences. You may need to change other words as well.

  a We rode on an elephant.

  b Mum said she had enjoyed it.

  c I should have bought something at the market.

2 Use some of the words from the box in part A to help you to write these negative sentences as positive sentences. You may need to change other words as well.

  a I have no money left.

  b I haven't taken any photographs.

  c I will never visit India again.

Writing

Advertisements

People who design advertisements make them attractive and eye-catching so you will stop and look. They have to consider:

What the advertisement looks like:
- colour – they may use bright colours, black and white, colours that blend together or contrasting colours
- layout – this needs to be clear and easy to read but eye-catching and interesting; the name of what is being advertised must be very noticeable
- illustration – this could be drawings, photographs or diagrams.

What the advertisement says:
- persuasive language – interesting language that states the good things about the item being advertised as strongly and dramatically as possible
- information – the advert needs to provide some information about the item being advertised.

A 1 Think carefully about a place you have visited on which you can base an advertisement for a colour magazine. This can be where you spent a holiday, a theme park, a museum, anywhere you like.

Plan your advertisement by making notes on the following before you begin:
- the place being advertised
- who the advertisement is aimed at
- how you will make it eye-catching
- what language you will use to persuade people to visit.

2 Do a first draft of your advertisement, thinking about how you will lay it out on the page, the colours you will use, the size of the writing, etc.

3 Write or word-process your final draft.

B Imagine you are running a travel agency, selling trips to the Moon, Mars or any planet of your choice. Design an advertisement that will persuade people to take a trip.

Fishing

Here is the back cover blurb of a book about fishing.

Angling for Beginners

C. Bream

Welcome to the world of fishing!

Fishing is the most popular pastime in Britain. More people go fishing than play any sport, including football, and no wonder! What other activity combines pitting your wits against the natural instincts of a creature you can't even see whilst allowing you to relax and enjoy pleasant and peaceful surroundings?

As you read on, you will realise that fishing involves far more than simply dangling a line into a river, pond, lake or reservoir and waiting for a fish to bite. This book will show you how to choose the equipment you need to get started, and how to use it. You will learn to identify the many different British freshwater fish, and to understand their individual habits and habitats and how to catch them. Above all, you will begin to get a feel for the tremendous enjoyment and excitement that come from a successful fishing trip.

GLOSSARY
angling fishing with a hook and line
reservoir a large lake supplying water to people's homes

 **Comprehension**

1. How does the writer feel about fishing?
2. What two reasons does the writer give for the popularity of fishing?
3. Explain one thing you would learn if you read the book.
4. Does the book blurb begin to persuade you that fishing might be enjoyable? Explain your reasons.

23 Windsor Crescent
Blaxington
BL6 7XZ

3rd October

RSPCA
Causeway
Horsham
West Sussex
RH12 1HG

Dear Sir/Madam

I have just been watching some people who are fishing in a lake near my house. I was absolutely disgusted by what I saw.

First, they were taking small, live worms, which they threaded onto fishing hooks, pushing the hooks right through their little bodies. Next, they swung them, on the end of the fishing rods, to dangle under the water waiting for a fish to bite them. Just because these creatures are small and can't make a noise doesn't mean they can't feel pain!

Then, when a fish did come alone and bite the bait, it would find a barbed hook would either get jammed in its lip, the roof of its mouth, or worse, right down its throat. If it struggled, which most fish did, the hook would dig in even deeper. It is horrible just to think of it.

Finally, the fish would be pulled from the water, gasping, have the hook removed, and then be put back into the river – only to have to suffer in the same way next time another angler wanted some fun!

Can you please tell me what the RSPCA, to whom I often give money, intends to do about such cruelty!

Yours faithfully

Nathan Lindsay

Nathan Lindsay

Comprehension

 1 How does the writer feel about fishing?
2 Explain in your own words one point that the writer makes to support his point of view.
3 Does this letter begin to persuade you that fishing is cruel? Explain your reasons.

 Choose either the book blurb or the letter and summarise:
- the writer's attitude to fishing
- the main points the writer makes.

Vocabulary
Homonyms

Remember, **homonyms** are words that are spelled and sound the same, but have different meanings. For example:
   I was absolutely disgusted by what I <u>saw</u>.
   I used a <u>saw</u> to cut the wood.

A Find each of the following homonyms in the two text extracts on pages 70 and 71. Use each homonym in a sentence of your own, giving it a different meaning from the one in the passage. The first one has been done to help you.

1 back   *I hurt my <u>back</u> when I fell over.*

2 right   3 line   4 trip   5 play

B Use a dictionary to help you find the different definitions of each homonym below. Write a sentence for each different meaning of each homonym. The first one has been done to help you.

1 hatch

   The eggs will <u>hatch</u> out soon.
   We passed the plates of food through the <u>hatch</u>.

2 bank   3 fine   4 fish   5 catch

Spelling
Root words, prefixes and suffixes

Remember, a **root word** is a word to which **prefixes** and **suffixes** can be added to make other words from the same word family. For example:
   h<u>ook</u>   h<u>ooking</u>   h<u>ooked</u>   h<u>ooks</u>   <u>un</u>hook   <u>un</u>hook<u>ed</u>
   <u>un</u>hook<u>ing</u>   <u>un</u>hook<u>s</u>

A Copy and complete the word webs for each these root words. Add more arrows if you can think of more words to add.

joyful   *remove*
  ⟵ (*joy*) ⟶   ⟵ (*move*) ⟶

B 1 In the text extracts on pages 70 and 71, find four other words that have roots. Copy the words and underline the root of each one. For example:

watching

2 Choose one of the root words you found in question 1. Write three sentences, each using a different word made from that root word. For example:

May I watch you fishing?
The watchful girl saw the fish.
I watched as she reeled it in.

Grammar

Word classes

 Word classes are sometimes called **parts of speech**.

Nouns, verbs, adjectives, adverbs, pronouns and conjunctions are all **word classes** – types of word. They are the main words that make up our language.

The small fish swam quickly and Sam missed it.

adjective — verb — adverb — verb — pronoun
noun — conjunction — proper noun

A 1 Write a short definition of each of the following parts of speech.

a a noun   b a verb   c an adjective
d an adverb   e a conjunction   f a pronoun

2 What is the difference between an ordinary noun and a proper noun?
3 Which part of speech tells us more about a noun?
4 Which part of speech tells us more about a verb?

B 1 Draw a table like the one below. Write each word from the box in the correct place on the table. Some words might go into more than one column.

Nouns	Pronouns	Adjectives	Verbs	Adverbs	Conjunctions

fish rod river Sam Uncle Brian I we it they blue big cruel frightened ran shouted digging fishing happily soon tomorrow quickly happiness which and but therefore Scotland

2 Write one sentence, using at least one word from each column of the table you drew in question 1.

Sentence construction
Using 'who' and 'which'

Remember, using **conjunctions** to join short sentences is an easy way to improve your writing. '**Who**' and '**which**' are useful conjunctions.

We use 'who' if we are writing about people. We usually use 'which' if we are writing about animals or things. For example:

I have just been watching some people <u>who</u> are fishing in a lake near my house ... they were taking small, live grubs and worms, <u>which</u> they threaded onto fishing hooks ...

Sometimes you might need to leave out one or two other words in the new sentence so it makes sense.

A Join each pair of sentences, using 'who' or 'which'.

1 This is my Uncle Brian. He likes fishing in the river.

2 He has bought a new hat. It prevents him getting sunburnt.

3 At the lake, we met some boys. They had some very expensive tackle.

4 Today, I caught two large fish. I threw them back before going home.

B Write two sentences of your own. Use 'who' in one sentence, and 'which' in the other. Underline the two parts of each sentence that are being joined.

Writing

Points of view

The book blurb on page 70 and the letter on page 71 were written by different people who have different **points of view** about fishing. The writer of the book concentrates on how much fun it is for the person fishing. The writer of the letter concentrates on how the grubs, worms and fish suffer.

To do a piece of writing putting across a particular point of view, you need to make notes on the points you wish to put across, then decide on the order in which to present them. First, briefly introduce the subject you are writing about, then present your points, one at a time, giving reasons to support each one.

A As well as sending his letter to the RSPCA, Nathan Lindsay also sent it to his local newspaper. Daniel Franks, a keen fisherman, read the letter and wrote to the newspaper to put his point of view. Imagine you are Daniel Franks and write the letter. You can use some of the ideas and information from the book blurb on page 70 but don't just copy from the extract.

B Imagine you are going to write the blurb for a book about your favourite sport or hobby. In the blurb, you need to explain what the sport is and why it is so enjoyable. Write the introduction in a way that would persuade the reader that the activity is very enjoyable, and which would persuade them to buy the book.

Check-up

Vocabulary

A Choose the **suffix** 'ade', 'ify' or 'ate' to complete each word.

1. persu___
2. cre___
3. imit___
4. magn___
5. complic___
6. inv___
7. terr___
8. rel___

B Use a dictionary to find the **definition** of each word.

1. peddle
2. ambition
3. derelict
4. turmoil

C Using a thesaurus, list at least three **synonyms** for each word below. Write the antonym of each word, if it has one.

1. quiet
2. awful
3. frail
4. thrifty

D Use each word in two sentences, the first using the word as a **noun**, the second using the word as a **verb**.

1. sail
2. run
3. fly
4. push

E Write a sentence using '**nice**'. Now write the sentence in three other ways without using 'nice'.

F Use a **suffix** from the box to make each word into an **adjective**.

1. wash
2. road
3. like
4. fun
5. trust

| y | able | ing | like | worthy |

G Complete each **simile**.

1. as steady as _____
2. as sharp as _____
3. as free as _____
4. as green as _____

H Use each **homonym** in some sentences of your own, to show its different meanings.

1. show
2. club
3. step
4. date
5. fire

Spelling

A
1 Write the **homophone** of each word.
   a sail   b flea   c pear   d whale   e shore
2 Choose three pairs of homophones from question 1 and use each word in a sentence of your own.

B Add 'ing' and 'ed' to each of these **verbs**.
1 jump   2 join   3 dream   4 roast   5 climb

C Write these past-tense verbs in the **present tense**.
1 thought   2 taught   3 sent   4 sung   5 fought

D Write these present-tense verbs in the **past tense**.
1 keep   2 pay   3 burst   4 know   5 grow

E For each word, write a **rhyming** word that has the same number of **syllables**.
1 funnel   2 bright   3 moaning   4 riddle   5 tower

F Choose 'al', 'le' or 'el' to complete each word.
1 medic___   2 humb___   3 accident___   4 shov___   5 padd___

G Sort these words into **alphabetical order**.
1 tarmac   street   cart   cobbles   stones
2 gravel   kerb   know   grabbing   knew

H Choose 'ge' or 'dge' to complete each word.
1 gara___   2 porri___   3 we___   4 enlar___   5 he___

I Write the **root word** to which the **suffix** 'ion' has been added to make each word below.
1 expression   2 observation   3 rejection   4 posession

Grammar

A Write each sentence again, putting in a synonym for the verb in colour.

1 The window shattered when the ball hit it.
2 They strolled through the park.
3 Peter grumbled because I was late.

B 1 Write these **present-tense** verbs using a **helper verb**.

    a we watch   b I help   c they build   d she makes

2 Write these **past-tense** verbs using a **helper verb**.

    a she collected   b I wrote   c you opened   d it melted

C Copy these sentences, adding **adjective phrases** to make them more interesting.

1 The old house, _____, stood at the top of the hill.
2 The boy, _____, rushed into the room.
3 The cake was removed from the oven, _____.

D Choose the correct **adjective** to complete each sentence.

1 In our team, Sanjay is the good/better/best batsman.
2 But Chris is a good/better/best bowler.
3 He is a fast/faster/fastest runner, too.

E Write two **adverbs** that could be used with each of these verbs.

1 laugh   2 walk   3 sleep   4 shout

F Copy the sentences below. Underline the **adverbs** and circle the **adjectives**.

1 You must tread carefully on this narrow path.
2 If you walk quickly, you will soon reach the huge forest.
3 I slipped on the muddy path and fell heavily.

Check-up

G 1 Make each of these sentences **plural**.

  a The dog chases the cat.
  b The cat climbs onto the fence.
  c The bird flies away quickly.
  d It escapes into a tree.

  2 Make each of these sentences **singular**.

  a Those dogs bark loudly.
  b The foxes hide in the bushes.
  c The birds peck the bread.
  d Jill's cats bask in the sun.

H Copy these sentences, choosing '**will**' or '**shall**' to fill each gap.

  1 I _____ open the window.
  2 They _____ go for a walk.
  3 You _____ enjoy yourself.
  4 I _____ have my own way!

I Copy the sentences below and label the **nouns, verbs, adjectives, adverbs, conjunction** and **pronoun**.

The hungry baby was crying loudly so the kind girl quickly made him a bottle of warm milk.

Punctuation and sentence construction

A Copy these sentences and add the missing **capital letters** and **punctuation** – commas, full stops, speech marks, apostrophes, question marks and exclamation marks.

  1 have you ever visited china asked karen
  2 were going to stay with eve in july
  3 dont touch that mike shouted

B Write these positive sentences as **negative** sentences.

  1 I like doing my homework.
  2 I was in the school play.
  3 I went on the school trip to France.

C Write each phrase in a shorter way, using a **possessive noun**.

1. the hat belonging to Tom
2. the stable of the horse
3. the kit belonging to the footballer
4. the bag belonging to Poppy

D Copy these sentences, adding the missing **apostrophes**.

1. Dads car isnt working.
2. Hes taking us on the bus.
3. Peters mum is collecting us.
4. We dont know when were leaving.

E Use conjunctions or commas to join these **clauses** to make single sentences.

1. it was a frosty morning   the sun shone brightly   the ice soon melted
2. the wind howled through the trees   the branches creaked   the leaves fell to the ground

Writing

A Write a newspaper report about a tiger escaping from a local zoo.

Think about:
- an eye-catching headline
- paragraphing
- facts
- opinions
- eye-witness accounts
- illustrations.

B Imagine there is a large playing field close to where you live but it has no play area and no goal posts. Write a letter to your local council to persuade them to put a play area or goal posts on the playing field.

Think about:
- how to address the letter
- how to begin your letter
- paragraphing
- how to end your letter.

C Imagine you are going away for a week and someone is going to come in and feed your cat and dog and water the plants. Write a list of instructions for them.

Think about:
- what they will need
- where they will find it
- what they should do.

Check-up